Tarik O'Regan

TRIPTYCH

(2004-5/2013)

Cantata for string orchestra and SSAA chorus

Score

NOVELLO

TRIPTYCH
Cantata for String Orchestra and SSAA Chorus

Duration

I.	*Threnody*	*c.* 5'
II.	*As We Remember Them*	*c.* 7'
III.	*From Heaven Distilled a Clemency*	*c.* 5'
	TOTAL	*c.* 17'

Instrumentation

SSAA chorus:
    soprano solo
String Orchestra:
    violin I
    violin II
    viola
    violoncello
    contrabass
    (min. 2.2.2.2.1 players)

Text

I. THRENODY

When death takes off the mask, [we] will know one another,
though diverse liveries [we] wear here make [us] strangers.
    William Penn (1644 – 1718),
        from 'Some Fruits of Solitude In Reflections And Maxims' (1682)

Tremblest thou when my face appears
To thee? Wherefore thy dreadful fears?
Be easy, friend; 'tis thy truest gain
To be far away from the sons of men.
I offer a couch to give thee ease:
Shall dreamless slumber so much displease?
    Muhammad Rajab Al-Bayoumi (dates unknown),
        from 'Death Speaks', translated by Arthur J. Arberry (1950)

To see a World in a Grain of Sand,
And a Heaven in a Wild Flower,
Hold Infinity in the palm of your hand,
And Eternity in an hour.
    William Blake (1757 – 1827),
        from 'Auguries of Innocence' (1808)

Behold, how good and how pleasant it is
for [people] to dwell together in unity.
    Psalm 133,
        from The Bible (King James Version, 1611)

II. AS WE REMEMBER THEM

In the rising of the sun and at its going down, we remember them.
In the blowing of the wind and in the chill of winter, we remember them.
In the opening buds and in the rebirth of spring, we remember them.
In the blueness of the sky and in the warmth of summer, we remember them.
In the rustling of the leaves and in the beauty of autumn, we remember them.
When [we're] weary and in need of strength, we remember them.
When [we're] lost and sick at heart, we remember them.
So long as we live, they too shall live, for they are part of us,
As we remember them.
> Roland B. Gittelsohn (1910 – 1995) [adapted],
> from 'The Gates of Repentance' (1978)

And the Heav'nly Quire stood mute,
And silence was in Heav'n.
> John Milton (1608 – 1674),
> from 'Paradise Lost', Book III (1667)

III. FROM HEAVEN DISTILLED A CLEMENCY

Each shall arise in the place where their life [spirit] departs.
> 'Bundahis-Bahman Yast'; Indian Bundahishn (ninth century) [adapted],
> from 'Sacred Books of the East', Volume 5, translated by Edward W. West (1860)

[So] Why then should I be afraid? I shall die once again to rise an angel blest.
> 'Masnavi i Ma'navi'; Mathwani of Jalalu-'d'Din Rumi (thirteenth century)
> [adapted],
> from 'Masnavi i Ma'navi', Book III, translated by Edward H. Whinfield (1898)

Our birth is but a sleep and a forgetting;
The Soul that rises with us, our life's Star,
Hath had elsewhere its setting.
And cometh from afar.
> William Wordsworth (1770 – 1850),
> from 'Ode: Intimations of Immortality' (1807)

Calm fell. From heaven distilled a clemency;
There was peace on earth, and silence in the sky.
> Thomas Hardy (1840 – 1928)
> from 'And There Was a Great Calm' – on the signing of the Armistice (1918)

General Notes

Triptych represents the concatenation of two commissions. Movement I was commissioned with funds from The RVW Trust for the inaugural concert of the Choir of London conducted by Jeremy Summerly in Christ Church, Spitalfields on 18 December 2004; the work, premiered as *Threnody*, was subsequently toured by the Choir to Jerusalem and the West Bank from 19 to 26 December 2004. Movements II and III, commissioned by Portsmouth Grammar School with financial support from the PRS Foundation, were premiered as *And There Was a Great Calm* in a contiguous version for lower strings and upper voices by the Portsmouth Grammar School Chamber Choir and the London Mozart Players in a concert at Portsmouth Anglican Cathedral on 13 November 2005 conducted by Nicolae Moldoveanu.

I gratefully acknowledge the assistance of Bruce Ruben and Judith Clurman, as well as that of my parents, with the collation of the texts.

Tarik O'Regan
New York, September 2005/January 2013

Full score NOV163152
Full score and parts available on hire from the publisher.
Also available for SATB chorus and strings
(vocal score NOV955691, study score NOV955702).

TRIPTYCH

Text: various (see notes)

Tarik O'Regan
(b. 1978)

I
Threnody

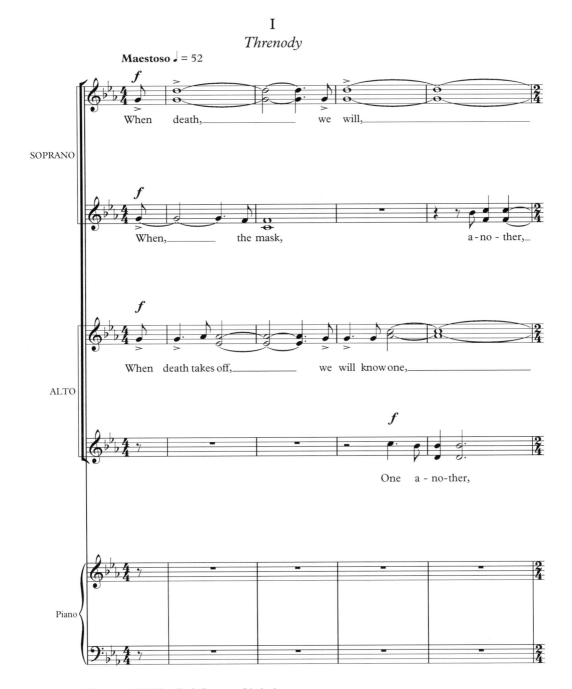

(sempre **p**)

Trem-blest thou when my face ap - pears____ To_____

Trem-blest thou when my face ap - pears____ To_____

_____ thee?_____ Where - fore_ thy

_____ thee?_____ Where - fore_ thy

6

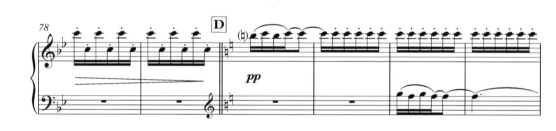

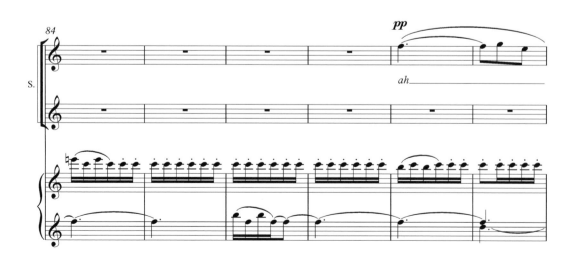

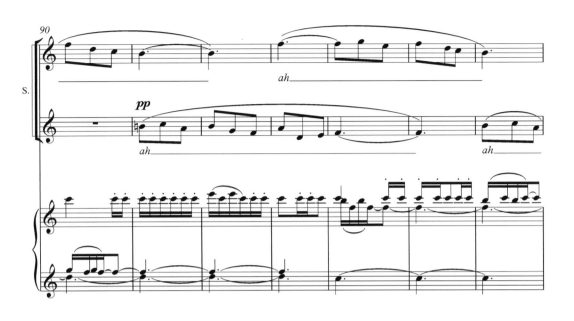

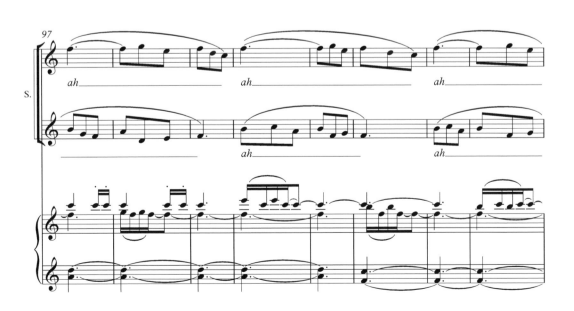

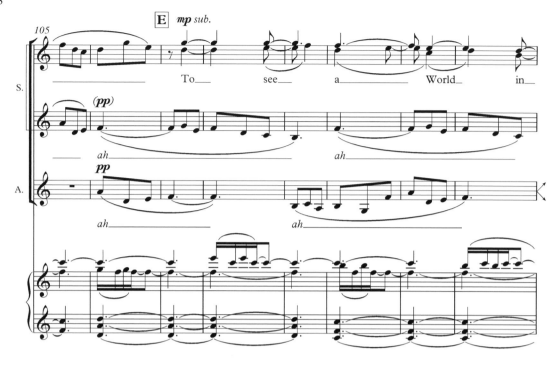

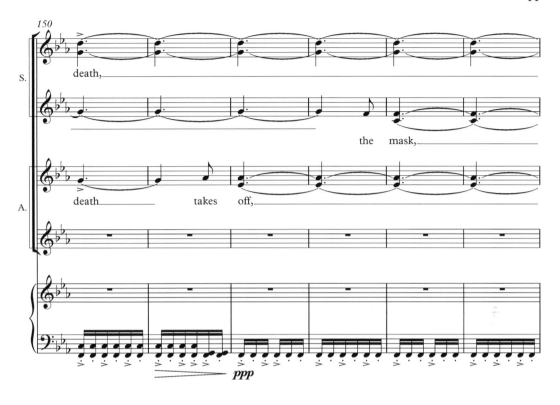

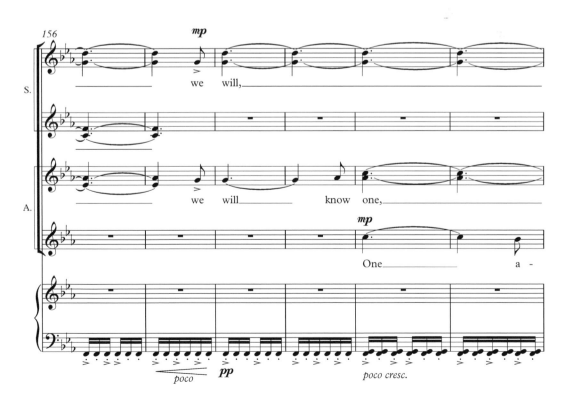

12

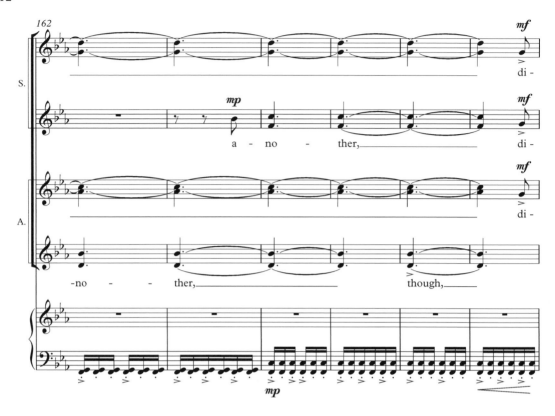

14

* Use bars 257-260 if performing *Threnody* as a single movement.
* Use bars 261-264 to continue with *As We Remember Them*.

II
As We Remember Them

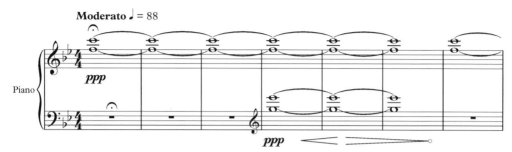

N.B. All the ties in the original string parts are shown. The pianist is advised to repeat the chords discreetly when needed. The original dynamics are also given, even when these are not practicable on the piano.

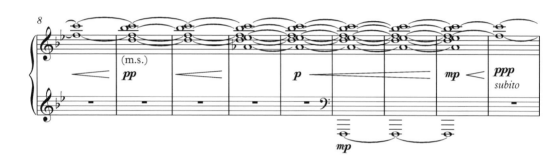

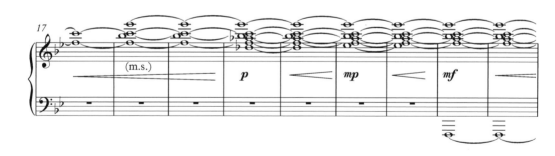

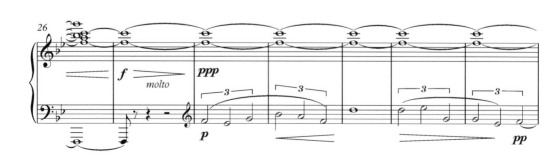

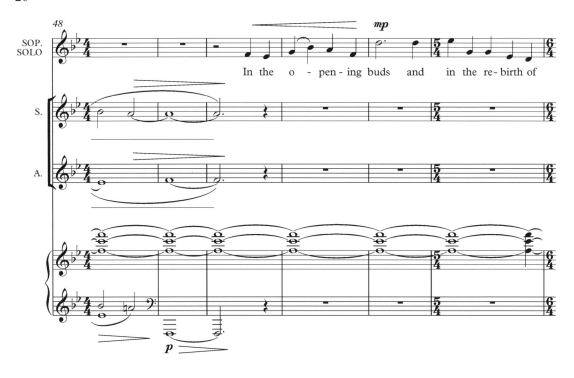

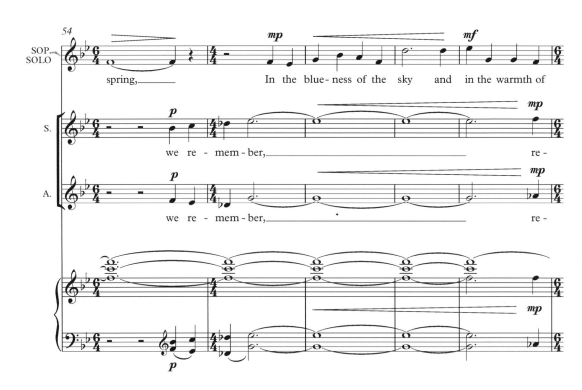

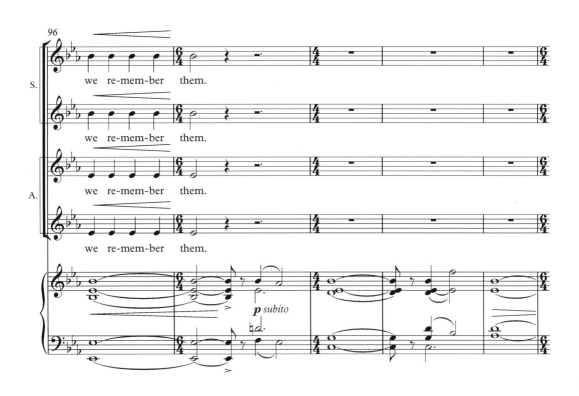

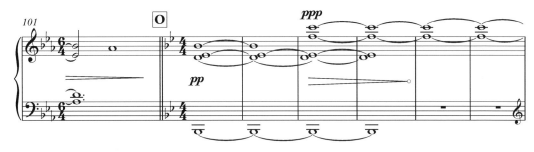

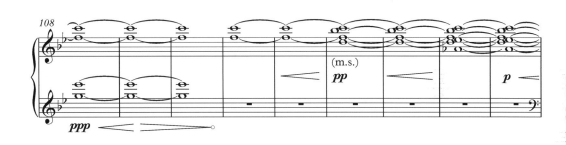

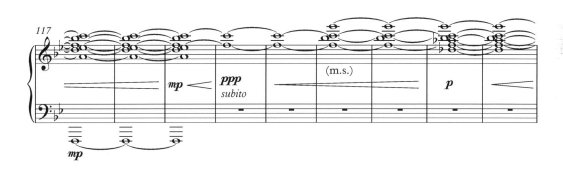

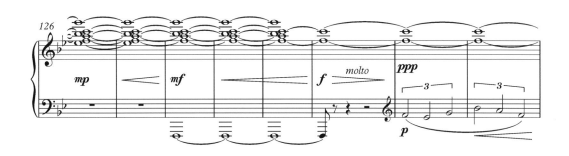

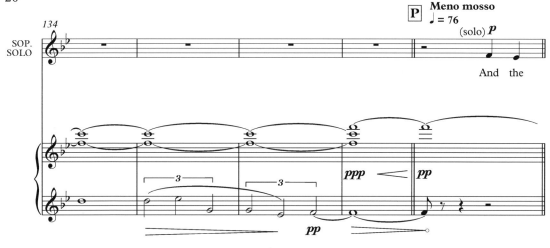

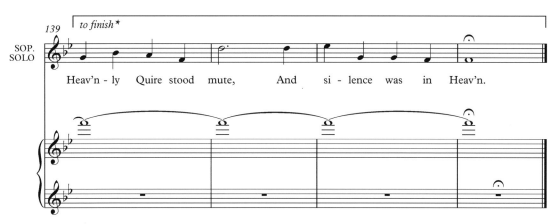

* Use bars 139-142 if perfoming *As We Remember Them* as a single movement.

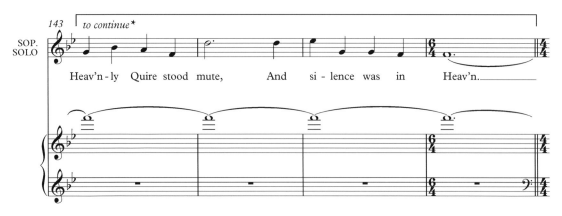

* Use bars 143-146 to continue with *From Heaven Distilled a Clemency*.

III

From Heaven Distilled a Clemency

* strings continue in quavers here

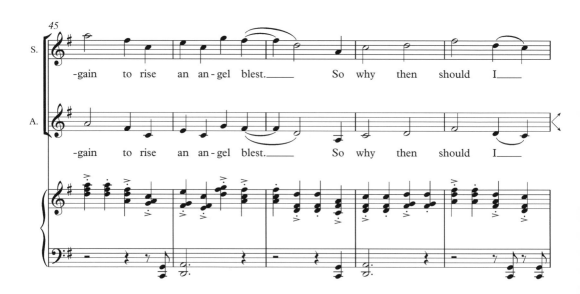

be__ a - fraid?__ I__ shall die once a - gain to rise an an - gel blest.__

be__ a - fraid?__ I__ shall die once a - gain to rise an an - gel blest.__

be__ a - fraid?__ I__ shall die once a - gain to rise an an - gel blest,__

an an - gel blest,__ an

32

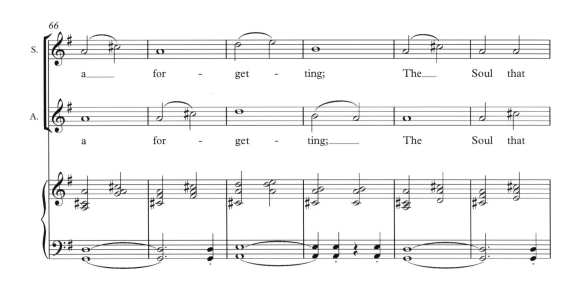

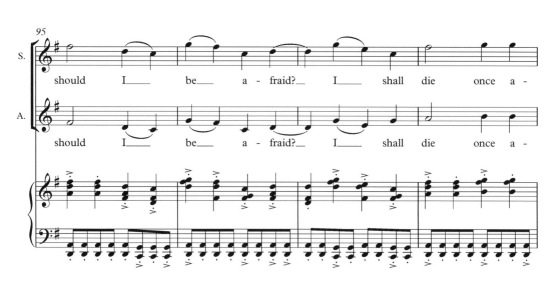

-gain   to rise   an   an - gel   blest._____

-gain   to rise   an   an - gel   blest._____

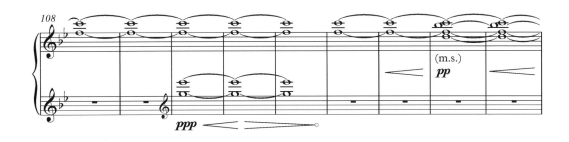

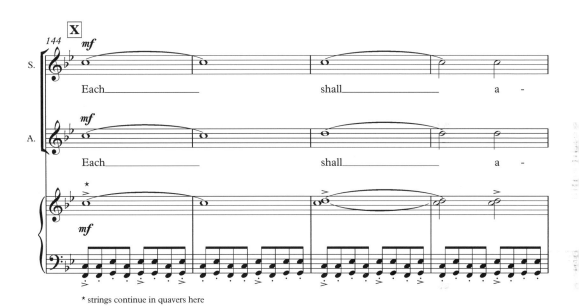

* strings continue in quavers here

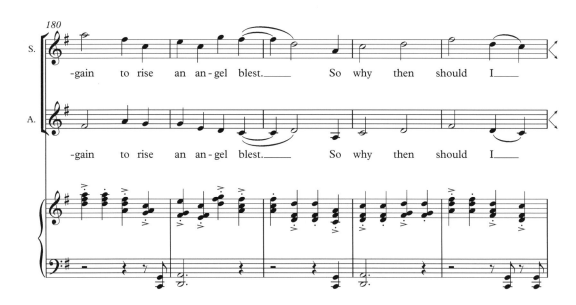

I__ shall die once a - gain to rise an an - gel blest.__

I shall die once a - gain to rise an an - gel blest.

I shall die once a - gain to rise an an - gel blest.__

I shall die once a - gain to rise an an - gel blest.__

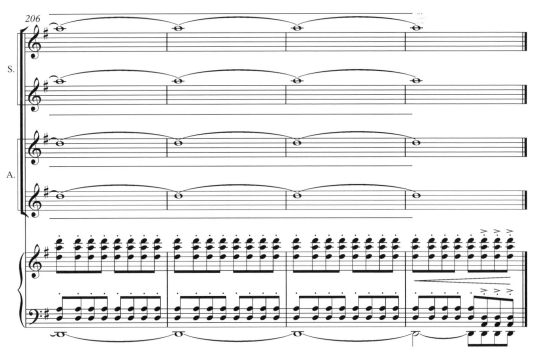